Cognitive Nourishment

Life-Changing Affirmations for the Savvy Teacher

Louise A. Chickie-Wolfe, PhD

The Brain Store, Inc.
4202 Sorrento Valley Blvd., Ste. B • San Diego, California 92121
E-mail: info@thebrainstore.com

Library of Congress Cataloging-in-Publication Data

Chickie-Wolfe, Louise A.
Cognitive nourishment : life-changing affirmations for the savvy teacher /
by Louise A. Chickie-Wolfe.
p.   cm.
Includes bibliographical references.
ISBN 1-890460-44-3 (pbk. : alk. paper)
1. Education—Quotations, maxims, etc. 2. Affirmations. I. Title.
PN6084.E38C48   2005
370--dc22

2005006446

Printed in the United States of America
3   5   7   9   10   8   6   4   2

Editor: Karen Miller   •   Book Designer: Jan Fenner

This book is printed on acid-free paper.

To my remarkable children, David and Dawn,
whose lives have so deeply enriched mine.

To my loving husband, Raleigh,
and our dear sons, Mike and Dave.

To my precious grandchildren:
Cereese, Aryanna, Elise, Nash, Hunter, Brianna, and Corey.

And to the throng of children and adults I have taught for the past
thirty years who give meaning, direction, and joy to my life
as a teacher, mentor, coach, and friend.

Table of Contents

Preface

This book was written while I was a doctoral student at Vanderbilt University. I awoke early one Saturday morning to begin a qualifying exam. I had cleared the entire day for this important work but, no matter how hard I tried, I couldn't get thoughts of teaching out of my mind. I decided I would just jot down my thoughts and be done with it in order to focus on my really important work. As I quickly listed a few ideas, I thought I might use them for an article some day. Then I noticed I would barely finish with one thought when another would emerge.

Although I had dreamed of writing a book since the time I was a little girl, I had no intentions of doing so that morning. But before I knew what actually happened, my thoughts turned into affirmations and the affirmations turned into the book you are holding. I typed with no awareness of the time until my puppy finally got my attention, needing to go outside. I was shocked when I opened the door and saw that it was dusk. I had been writing the entire day! My thoughts had just gushed out, nonstop. That moment was when I first realized how much teaching had changed my life for the better.

The second time I had this powerful realization was after I had earned my Ph.D. and had been working for several years as an educational/behavioral consultant for several school districts. It seemed that the higher up the ladder I went in education, the farther I moved away from directly serving kids. Though my consulting work was challenging and satisfying, I found I missed teaching very much—I was hungry for the interaction and personal contact I used to get on a daily basis. To the surprise of many, I rolled up my sleeves and returned to the classroom. That was five years ago, and I have never once regretted that decision. Teaching is hard work, but it nourishes you in a way that other professions do not. There isn't a day that goes by that I don't laugh and celebrate the fact that I am lucky to be a teacher! ■

Introduction

This powerful little book is for all people who teach. It is written in first person so that teachers can read these statements and apply the ideas to their own particular teaching situations. It applies equally to male and female teachers in all areas of teaching and it represents my dynamic philosophy of teaching that took thirty years to develop.

Not only is this book extremely valuable for teachers, it is also important to principals, superintendents, educational specialists, counselors, social workers, therapists, coaches, mentors, tutors, school board members, student teachers, and university professors involved in teacher education programs. It is a useful tool for anyone who teaches others in any capacity.

Research indicates that people who make repeated cognitive affirmations can actually change the way their brains function—the positive and negative messages we tell ourselves influence our own physiology.[1] Emile Coue, the 19th century French professor, became a pioneer of affirmation techniques with his famous affirmation, "Every day in every way I am getting better and better."[2] The results of his work suggest that affirmations are powerful tools that can bring about major changes in the subconscious mind. Brain research indicates that affirmations can reset the brain through suggestions and that the brain processes suggestions or affirmations as being real. This inner speech serves as the principle vehicle of thought and self-direction.[3] Positive thoughts can even improve our health![4]

Cognitive affirmations nourish our thoughts and beliefs. These powerful statements are truly life-changing. When repeated daily, cognitive affirmations establish a positive mindset that guides our behavior toward goal attainment. ▪

What Are Cognitive Affirmations?

Cognitive affirmations are positive statements about your beliefs; they are self-statements, or self-talk, that influence your brain to act in a desired way, like helping you strive for excellence and reach your goals. Each affirmation in this book is followed by an elaboration, a short paragraph that explains the affirmation in more detail.

As you read this book, take the time to visually imagine these statements as they apply to you. Try to actually see yourself putting the statements into action. Accept any statements that represent your beliefs and add any thoughts of your own that affirm your personal commitment to teaching. Directions for writing your own affirmations and blank pages at the end of the book are provided for this express purpose.

It has been a tremendous learning experience for me to formulate and describe my teaching philosophy through cognitive affirmations. Taking the time to compose and physically write your beliefs in the form of affirmations will help you develop your own positive philosophy for teaching others. ■

Your Brain Believes What You Tell It

I have prominently displayed in my classroom a poster that says, "Your Brain Believes What You Tell It." There isn't a day that goes by that I don't remind my students of this important truth.

The brain believes what we tell it and reacts accordingly. Amazingly, an idea doesn't even have to be said aloud for the brain to be solidly programmed in powerful ways to believe the message. We only have to *think* about something for it to come true! This is the reason we maintain fears and phobias even when we understand that they are irrational and even when they wreak havoc with our lives. It also explains why people can experience superhuman strength when they face crisis situations.

When students think negative thoughts such as, "Oh, this is terrible! I'm going to fail this test," they decrease the likelihood of doing their best work. Programming their brain in this negative way often sabotages their performance. But telling the brain positive things can have powerful outcomes in the same way that telling the brain negative things influences it negatively.[5] When students make positive statements such as, "I studied hard and I know I'm going to do a great job on this test," they increase their chances of doing just that.

In the same way, your brain will respond positively if you read the cognitive affirmations in this book daily and program your brain to be successful. Like the brain of a student, the brain of a teacher is strongly influenced by what it is told. With cognitive affirmations, you can turn any negative thoughts you may be having into a positive program for success and growth. This book will help you accomplish that goal. ■

Brain-Compatible Instruction

Though affirmations have been around for a long time, our understanding of how they change the neural network within the brain and our appreciation of their power within the body of knowledge in brain research is relatively new. Despite its newness, however, much research supports the fact that teachers can create an atmosphere within the classroom that invites learning through brain-compatible instruction.[6] Reframing self-statements through cognitive affirmations will open new neural pathways that allow us to stretch our abilities and achieve success far greater than ever imagined.

Still, the idea isn't new. Professional athletes are taught by personal trainers to use cognitive restructuring (e.g., affirmations) to develop self-affirming beliefs and challenge negative and counterproductive thinking.[7] Sports psychologists consult with major league teams all the time to instill in players' minds the thought, "I can do it." Winning coaches like Don Shula stress positive beliefs as the basis of success.[8] Sales, motivation, religion, and time management professionals all use the power of positive affirmations and positive thinking.[9] Even a children's book, *The Little Engine That Could*, espouses the power of telling oneself, "I think I can."[10]

Now teachers understand that an absence of threat allows the brain to achieve levels of higher-order thinking. Conversely, stress, anxiety, or fear immobilizes students, making it impossible for them to think clearly and effectively. The end results of threat are often academic and social failure, frustration, behavior problems, and increased drop-out rates from school. Putting the brain at ease through brain-compatible instruction can reverse this trend. Because the affirmations in this book are brain-based, they are better able to help any teacher think positive thoughts about how and what they teach. ■

The Nature of the Message

The cognitive affirmations and subsequent elaborations in this book remind us of the joys and responsibilities of teaching that are often forgotten in the day-to-day demands of our profession. We are routinely asked to do more with less. Effective teaching strategies have been blended with positive affirmational statements, making this a book of methodology as well as inspiration. It is appropriate for teachers of students of all ages (preschool through college) and of all ability levels (regular, special, and gifted). It offers a unique opportunity for personal and professional growth.

Hopefully, *Cognitive Nourishment* will extinguish the fire of "burnout" for veteran teachers who need support and motivation to persevere and excel. For the new teacher, this book provides needed information and valuable guidance. For everyone who considers its message, this book offers inspiration that will refuel and inspire us. The message in this book also speaks to parents with the desire to have their child's teacher embrace its philosophy. For the parent who is looking for that very special gift for the teacher, this is definitely it! ■

Practice Makes Perfect

Reading thirty-four affirmations in a row can be overwhelming; selecting one affirmation to concentrate on each day will enable you to use this book more effectively. Keep the book on your desk as a visual reminder to repeat a selected affirmation several times throughout the day. Doing so will keep you focused on one area of professional growth at a time. As you repeat the affirmations and read the elaborations, you will be reprogramming your brain to think positively about your profession and the ways you interact with your students and others.

Henry Thoreau wrote in *Walden*, "I know of no more encouraging fact than the unquestionable ability of man to elevate his life by a conscious endeavor." Making an intentional effort to repeat positive affirmations about teaching is one such endeavor that will surely bring about the success we seek as educators. ■

Conclusion

I t is my hope that you will face your students with renewed vigor, improved skills, and increased enthusiasm after using these materials, that you will experience the passion and rewards that teaching can bring, and that you will fully realize that you are incredibly lucky to be a teacher!

Whereas some teachers just *hope* for positive life changes, those who use cognitive affirmations become inspired to *produce* their own future. The savvy teacher knows that a daily dose of cognitive affirmations will nourish the brain and cause it to flourish.

■ ■ ■

References

1 Foss, Laurence (Summer, 1995). Animal brain vs. human mind-brain: The dilemma of mind-body medicine. *Advances: The Journal of Mind-Body Health*, 11, 57–70.

2 Coue, Emile (1923). *How to Practice Suggestion and Autosuggestion*. Whitefish, MT: Kessinger Publishing.

3 Brown, Trevor C. (Winter, 2003). The effect of verbal self-guidance training on collective efficacy and team performance? *Personnel Psychology*, 56(4), 935–64.

4 Spiegel, D. (1991). A psychological intervention and survival time of patients with metastatic breast cancer. *Advances: The Journal of Mind-Body Health*, 7, 3.

5 Bandura, Albert (1997). *Self-Efficacy: The Exercise of Control*. New York: Freeman.

6 Jensen, Eric (1998). *Introduction to Brain-Compatible Learning*. San Diego, CA: The Brain Store.

7 Williams, J. (1998). *Applied Sport Psychology: Personal Growth to Peak Performance*. London: Mayfield.

8 Blanchard, Ken & Shula, Don (2001). *The Little Book of Coaching: Motivating People to Be Winners*. New York: HarperBusiness.

9 Peale, Norman Vincent (1996). *The Power of Positive Thinking*. New York: Fawcett Columbine.

10 Piper, W. (1930). *The Little Engine that Could*. New York: Platt & Munk.

Additional Reading

Bloch, Douglas (1993). *Positive Self-Talk for Children: Teaching Self-Esteem through Affirmations: A Guide for Parents, Teachers, and Counselors*. New York: Bantam.

The Affirmations and Elaborations

I Believe in the Inherent Worth of Each Student.

E very child committed to my care has worth and importance. My students don't have to prove that to me. I value them as human beings and I realize that their parents have entrusted them to my care. I will treat my students just as I would want a child of my own to be treated.

I Make a Difference in the Lives of My Students.

My students remember with satisfaction the time we spend together. Each student gains in knowledge, confidence, and ability during our interactions. I take students to places of learning they have never been to before. Each student benefits from our paths having crossed and looks back with pride on their accomplishments and growth.

I Create a Safe and Friendly Atmosphere in My Classroom.

Regardless of what my students face outside of school, they want to be in our classroom. They know that they are important; they learn to help one another and share the joys and frustrations of growing up. They are brave and confident. My students know that their opinions matter and that they are treated fairly. They build and maintain friendships with each other and with me. We laugh and cry and learn together, and our classroom is a magical place.

Life-Changing Affirmations for the Savvy Teacher

I Smile a Lot and Am Very Positive in My Work.

My students like being around me. They are able to count on me and reflect on school as a happy experience. Because enthusiasm and joy are contagious, they also laugh a lot and are optimistic about their future. They see that I love my work and they love theirs.

I Say Exactly What I Mean and Mean Exactly What I Say.

I think carefully before I speak. I am clear and concise, and do not make idle threats. My students are able to count on me to be predictably fair when they are behaving appropriately as well as when they are not. When they lose control, my students count on me to help them regain it. I keep my promises. I am not vague because my students need to understand exactly what I mean. When I say it, I mean it. When I say I care about them, I do. When I say I will correct unacceptable behavior, I will. When I say my students can count on me, they can.

I Am Fair and Considerate of My Students' Feelings.

I treat my students fairly, but not necessarily equally, for some require more assistance at times than others. I care about my students and how they feel. I speak to them in private about sensitive issues and I understand when they are having a rough day. I respect my students and their families.

I Am Creative and Competent.

Although I don't know everything there is to know about education, I am well trained and capable of performing my duties effectively. Each day of a teacher's life is different from any of the others; I love this unpredictable nature of my work. I thrive on creatively teaching the same idea in novel ways. Every time I present a lesson, I improve the way I do it. I continually seek new materials, ideas, and activities for my classroom. I am thrilled each time the "light bulb" lights for one of my students. This "A-Ha" moment brings me joy.

I Realize that Teaching Is a Profession of Utmost Importance.

When I look around, I am hard-pressed to find another career that is as important to the world as teaching. I have seen many gifted teachers leave the field of teaching to find more lucrative positions and this saddens me. I am very proud of what I do and I realize that the future rests on my shoulders. I do not recoil from this awesome responsibility—I welcome it.

I Believe that Children Are Our Most Important Natural Resource.

L ook around. The social problems facing this nation are horrendous: poverty, abuse, oppression, divorce, illness, illiteracy, homelessness, prejudice, drugs, crime, suicide, violence, fear, terrorism, isolation. Children are having children. Children are killing children—with no regard for the value and quality of life. Will values, morals, and spirituality become extinct? Who will put this world back in order? Who calms the stormy seas? Who makes a difference and rights the wrongs?

My students do!

I Am a Lifelong Learner and My Students Know It.

Cognitive Nourishment

Because I value knowledge, I model that belief in my classroom. My students see me reading to gain information and for enjoyment. I show, through example, that writing is a worthwhile skill. I use mathematics to make sense of my surroundings and I solve problems and resolve conflicts to illustrate the importance of knowledge. I continue to seek new information about many topics and I allow my students to join me in this exciting pursuit. I demonstrate my enthusiasm for learning new things and I prove each day that I have many more questions than answers.

Life-Changing Affirmations for the Savvy Teacher

I Am Organized and Plan Ahead.

I invest the time necessary to do my job well. I plan my lessons carefully and organize my materials ahead of time. I stay focused on the goals and do not become sidetracked with irrelevant tasks. I think about my students and their strengths and I teach accordingly.

*I Believe that Teaching
Is Satisfying
and Rewarding.*

Cognitive Nourishment

Success is doing what you love and loving what you do. That's how I feel about teaching. Little can compare to the sense of satisfaction a teacher feels when students master concepts previously foreign to them. Every squeal that ends with, "Oh, I get it!" brings a feeling of pride that is difficult to describe. Students are so uninhibited and refreshing! Warm hugs come from the little ones with a sincere, "I love you." Pictures drawn just for me decorate my refrigerator at home. Letters and visits come from former students and are rewards few people ever enjoy. Sometimes I am trusted enough for students to reveal their real selves to me— selves others do not often get to see. Teaching gives me a deep sense of satisfaction.

*I Am Not the Same
Teacher I Was Yesterday
Because Each Day
I Learn and
Experience More.*

Cognitive Nourishment

With the passage of time, I become more and more competent. I discover more about myself and learn new ways of reaching children. I am in a place today that I have never been before. I have never known as much as I know today. Each experience adds wisdom that I carry into my classroom and share with my students. The future holds such promise for us all.

*I Remember How Much
It Hurts to Fail and
I Am Patient and
Understanding with
Students' Difficulties.*

When students are struggling, I am there to help them in the same way my family and friends are there to help me when things do not go well. I am sensitive to the feelings of my students. I let them know it is natural to make mistakes and to not have all the answers. I empathize with their plight and do all I can to help them overcome their frustrations or endure their pain. For some of my students, school is a frightening place where just answering a question means taking a risk for which they are ill-prepared. Others are impulsive and continually break the rules. Some cannot read well or pass tests no matter how hard they study. Many students have no friends. Whatever difficulties my students experience, I am there to assist them.

I Do Not Take
Personally Anything
Said to Me in Anger
by a Student.

I know that remaining objective during a problem is important. I know, too, that youngsters can become upset with their teachers for a variety of reasons, many over which we have no control. When students lose control, I am there to calm them down and help them regain their composure. I remember that much of what they say at a time when they are most angry is the truth turned upside down. "I hate you and I hate this school!" shouted in anger often means a student does care but feels somehow betrayed. I accept, with no animosity, any apology in whatever form it is given. After consequences are served by the student, I wipe the slate clean and harbor no ill-feelings. Then, I let the student know that all is forgiven and that our relationship continues unshaken.

I Am Consistent and Knowledgeable in My Field.

I am mindful of school rules and consistently enforce them. Consistency yields predictability, so my students feel secure. I continue to pursue knowledge in my respective field of education so that I am able to provide a strong program and a valuable experience for my students.

I Know My Students'
Abilities and I Have
Realistic Expectations
for Each of Them.

Cognitive Nourishment

I carefully observe, monitor, assess, and interact with my students to gather information about their strengths, weaknesses, deficits, and interests. I uphold high standards that are obtainable for my students on a consistent basis. I know how and on what levels my students are functioning. I ask them to do meaningful tasks that they are capable of doing and for which they are prepared. I appreciate their limited time and avoid busy work that serves no purpose in accomplishing their goals. I "scaffold" their learning activities to stretch their ability in systematic and sequential steps. I have realistic academic and social expectations for all of my students.

My Students and I Become a Family.

Just as with our own families, students in my classroom feel supported, encouraged, and cared about by their classmates and by me. We work together, all for one and one for all, cooperatively and with respect for one another. All students contribute to our classroom's success by using their strengths and sharing their talents and interests. We understand and appreciate our multiple intelligences and do not expect everyone to learn or think alike. Being made fun of, being bullied, being left out, or being gossiped about is unheard of among our classroom family. All students' opinions matter to each of us, especially when they do not match our own. Every student knows he or she is important to the well-being of the entire group. When students are absent, they are missed. Our family atmosphere gives my students a sense of belonging and an identity that sets the stage for learning.

I Celebrate Every Milestone—Even the Smallest Ones.

I believe in celebration. Success doesn't come only at the end of the school year—it happens every day and should be measured and recognized one little piece at a time. I do not wait until the final result but find joy in every manifestation of growth as it occurs. This discovery inspires me to persevere and enjoy each day.

I Help My Students Find Academic and Personal Success.

I individualize as much as possible to accommo-date the wonderful diversity in my classroom. After I teach, I check for understanding before assigning work. I re-teach when students do not understand. I tell and show at the same time. I demonstrate and then watch to be sure students are getting it right. I provide lots of practice, enriched opportunities, hands-on experiences, and specific feedback. I am a good listener. Working with students in this way just about guarantees their academic and personal success.

I Model Honesty and Dependability.

I am truthful with my students and their parents. I am honest in my dealings with other professionals. My students and colleagues are able to depend on me because I consistently do my job to the best of my ability.

I Encourage My Students to Think.

Cognitive Nourishment

My students are thinkers. They are reflective and thoughtful participants in our classroom. I help them understand that their first thought is not always their best thought, so speed is not the desired outcome. While some students are thinking carefully, the others practice patience. I increase my wait time to give students the opportunity to think through their responses. I call on someone else only when my student gives me the signal to do so. Then, I let that student choose a classmate to call on for some help. I teach my students about the brain and how it functions. They understand about thinking from the inside out. I encourage them to drink more water, eat healthy food, and get plenty of sleep. I make sure the lesson being taught is relevant and challenging so that it stretches my students' minds into higher levels of thinking.

I Enjoy the Diversity of My Students.

I love the diversity my students bring to the classroom and I am continually challenged to meet their unique needs. How boring it would be if all of my students looked exactly alike! I would not be able to tell them apart. If they all learned in the same way and at the same rate, it would save a lot of time, but teaching would become mechanical and boring. My class is a microcosm of the world outside. Because my students learn to get along with each other in the classroom, they are more prepared to accept and enjoy the differences they find in people now and in the future.

I Share Positive Moments from My Class with Colleagues.

I know all too well that teaching is a very difficult job. For some educators, unfortunately, teaching can be lonely and unfulfilling. With this reality in mind, I refrain from complaining in the teacher's lounge or lunchroom even when I am having a terrible day. (Yes, it happens to all of us.) Instead, I find a positive moment and share it with a colleague. I am in the habit of asking others to share their good news about students with me as well. This upbeat sharing brings us joy and often laughter, which transforms difficult days into pleasant ones.

I Know How the Brain Works Best and I Teach Accordingly.

Cognitive Nourishment

I give my students periodic "brain breaks" to provide the time necessary for them to make personal meaning out of what was just presented. I know that lecturing to students for long periods of time actually makes learning harder. I get my students up, moving around, and actively involved in their own learning.

I model and encourage drinking adequate amounts of water throughout the school day because I know the brain functions best when it is adequately hydrated.

I provide music for my students as they complete various tasks. I also sing with them because I know this activates many different parts of the brain, which facilitates learning.

I Make Personal Connections with My Students.

Students learn easily when they feel connected to their teacher. I facilitate good relationships in many ways. I send students postcards at the end of the summer to introduce myself and plant the seed that this will be a fantastic year. I make sure to learn and use their names right away. I use eye contact, smiles, and thumbs-up gestures, and reach out personally to my students. I make a point to learn something unique about each one. This knowledge may involve their family, talents, interests, past experiences, or extra-curricular activities. When I treat students in this way, we establish a bond and our discussions become pleasant and comfortable. My students know I am approachable.

I Help My Students Make Personal Connections to What They Study.

I help my students make personal connections to what they study so they understand its relevance. Learning does not happen in isolation. Everything we comprehend is tied to something we already understand. We share prior knowledge about the topic. Then, we analyze how this new learning relates to them, their lives, their class, their community, their state, their nation, and their world. To their amazement, we make links from new vocabulary to words they already know. We study the past and discuss current news by relating those events to their lives. In this way, students appreciate that they are part of a much larger world and they understand that everything they do and fail to do affects others.

I Incorporate Service Projects into My Teaching.

Children need to be taught to give back to their communities. Their personal focus should be on "giving" rather than on "getting." Regardless of age, children can benefit from participation in projects that are designed to help others. There are many ways that children can learn to make a difference in society. Being a part of an organized effort to assist others teaches the importance of civic responsibility and instills confidence and pride. These experiences establish a pattern of caring that often inspires a lifelong spirit of volunteerism and service to others.

Life-Changing Affirmations for the Savvy Teacher

I Welcome Change and Handle It Easily.

Cognitive Nourishment

The life of a teacher is ever-changing. In education, the pendulum of trends, jargon, and "cutting edge" programs constantly swings from one direction to the other…and then back again. I am asked to serve on committees, attend meetings, plan school-related events, maintain accurate records, keep the school nurse, psychologist, speech therapist, and principal all appraised of students in need of attention, and find an extra desk for the new student— all while imparting the best education I can provide to each of my students (with different levels of ability, self-control, and motivation). New challenges come with every new class. The one thing that stays the same in teaching is that it constantly changes. For this reason, I comfortably anticipate change and view it not only as routine, but I welcome it as necessary for growth…mine and my students.

*I Seek and Find Peace
in My Workplace
as I Help Build
a Better World.*

I successfully deal with the many stresses of my job. I stay positive and happy. I focus my thoughts and attention on what is truly important about my work and I remember that what I do makes a profound difference in the world. Each day I do one positive thing, big or small, for *myself* in each of these three categories: People, Profession, and Personal. For People, I might call a friend I haven't spoken to in a while, give a compliment to someone, or be a good listener. For Profession, I might read a journal article I've been interested in or get a stack of papers graded. For Personal, I will do something nice for myself like take a walk or listen to my favorite CD. When I accomplish one thing in each of the three "P" categories each day, I feel balanced, fulfilled, and satisfied. It is then that I find peace in who I am and what I do.

I Respect My Students
and They Respect Me.

Cognitive Nourishment

Discipline becomes manageable when I respect my students and they respect me. Each time I keep my word, it is like receiving a deposit of trust from others in a special bank account. Over time, I build up quite a large holding. When a problem or misunderstanding occurs between me and another person, it is as though that person makes a withdrawal from my account. As long as there have been lots of regular deposits of trust between us, we can withstand a withdrawal—even a fairly large one. Respect allows students to do as we ask, even when they would rather not. Respect allows relationships to endure despite our difficulties. Respect allows me to overlook the short-comings of others and to focus instead on their worth.

My Students and I Have Fun Together.

My students and I find something to laugh about every day in my classroom. We consciously develop a sense of humor that filters out many of the problems of the day. School is fun, and my students and I are fortunate enough to realize it.

My Students and I Learn Together.

I learn as much from my students as they learn from me because teaching is reciprocal. In any given lesson, I shift back and forth repeatedly between teaching and learning.

I am incredibly lucky to be a teacher!

Your Own Personalized Affirmations

Guidelines for Writing Your Own Affirmations

As you read this book and examine your teaching situation, you'll probably think of additional affirmations that you feel would be useful to you. Writing down these affirmations will help you benefit from them. Remember that affirmations are *positive* statements that reflect your own personal commitment to teaching. Each affirmation should be stated in first person and written in the present tense (even if you aren't doing them yet). Some helpful starting phrases are "I am," "I value," or "I can."

Also, be on the lookout for any negative self-statements that you may catch yourself thinking or saying. Transform them by turning them around to make them positive. For example, if you often hear yourself saying, "I'll never get all of this finished today," you might write an affirmation that says, "I finish all of my important work."

For the second part of creating an affirmation, write out an elaboration that expands your ideas in positive terms by describing what it means to *you*. This process really personalizes the affirmations as you take time to individualize these statements to your own situation.

To write an elaboration for the example affirmation, "I finish all of my important work," you might write about how you break large projects into separate categories and then decide what should be completed right away and what you can deal with later.

Focus on your beliefs and the aspects of teaching you value most. Tap into your emotions as you write each affirmation and elaboration. Emotions activate the brain, stimulate learning, and promote memory. Involving your emotions will also invigorate and refuel you as you dig deep to find the passion that great teaching is all about. Teaching nourishes the mind and changes the heart for the better, so **always remember that you are incredibly lucky to be a teacher!**

And good luck. ▪

Workspace for Writing Your Own Affirmations and Elaborations

_____

_____

_____

_____

_____

_____

_____

_____

_____

_____

_____

_____

_____

_____

_____

_____

Workspace for Writing Your Own Affirmations and Elaborations

Workspace for Writing Your Own Affirmations and Elaborations

Workspace for Writing Your Own Affirmations and Elaborations

_____

_____

_____

_____

_____

_____

_____

_____

_____

_____

_____

_____

_____

_____

_____

_____

About the Author

Louise A. Chickie-Wolfe has been a teacher for thirty years. She has taught regular education, gifted children, and students with serious learning and behavior problems. Her experience covers elementary, middle school, high school, and college levels. Louise has also informed and motivated educators and parents at workshops across the country. An adjunct professor at Purdue University Calumet for more than twenty-five years, she earned her doctorate degree at George Peabody College of Vanderbilt University in Special Education and Human Development. She trained and supervised student teachers at Peabody College, where she also taught courses in special education and managing academic and social behavior in the classroom. Named Outstanding Teacher of the Year by the Indiana chapter of the Council for Exceptional Children and again by the Inland Steel/Ryerson Foundation, Louise has developed a philosophy that is sensitive, positive, and successful.

Learn from
Top Education Experts
at Learning Brain Expo

The Brain Store hosts Learning Brain Expo, a biannual brain and learning conference for educators and administrators. Visit **www.brainexpo.com** to find out how you can

- boost student achievement through applied brain research
- bridge the gap between neuroscience and the classroom
- translate research into real learning solutions
- learn strategies to help every learner succeed
- earn CEU and graduate credit

Two easy ways to stay up to date!

- Send an e-mail to **info@thebrainstore.com** to be notified about new products and special offers!
- Visit **www.thebrainstore.com** and click **FREE Teaching Tips**.

Best-Selling Titles
from **The Brain Store**

Resources for Growing Minds ®

Classroom Activators:
64 Novel Ways to Energize Learners
By Jerry Evanski, EdD, Foreword by Eric Jensen

Put a new twist on teaching and training practices and invigorate your learners with this handy, pocket-sized guide. Each of the three sections—Environmental, Instructor, and Student—presents specific state-changing activities and the brain research behind them. Strategies can be adapted for any age group, from primary to adult. You'll be amazed how simple changes in the way you present material or arrange the classroom can capture students' interest and keep them focused. Shake things up and see results immediately! ©2004 • 141 pages • #1657

Write Brain Write: Proven Success Tools for
Developing the Writer in Every Student
By Anne Hanson

When it comes to teaching writing, what should educators know about the brain and learning? This valuable resource will help you develop effective and passionate student writers in classrooms of any type at any level. From descriptive and narrative writing techniques to expository and persuasive writing strategies, Anne Hanson advocates a "coaching" approach—a quarter-by-quarter game plan that addresses planning, assessment, and curriculum selection. Learn why seating matters, how to think outside the textbook box, what significant changes impact present-day learners' brains, how tapping into the past fuels the fires of the mind, and which real-life applications ensure progress. Develop a classroom full of brilliant writers with this proven, effective approach! ©2002 • 215 pages • #1416